Inside or Outside

Where's Eddie?

Daniel Nunn

Illustrations by Steve Walker

Chicago, Illinois

www.capstonepub.com
Visit our website to find out more information about Heinemann-Raintree books.

To order:
Phone 800-747-4992
Visit www.capstonepub.com to browse our catalog and order online.

© 2013 Raintree is an imprint of Capstone Global Library, LLC
Chicago, Illinois

All rights reserved. No part of this publication may be reproduced or transmitted in any form or by any means, electronic or mechanical, including photocopying, recording, taping, or any information storage and retrieval system, without permission in writing from the publisher.

Edited by Dan Nunn, Rebecca Rissman, and Sian Smith
Designed by Joanna Hinton-Malivoire
Picture research by Mica Brancic
Originated by Capstone Global Library, Ltd.
Production by Victoria Fitzgerald
Printed in the United States of America in
North Mankato, MN. 012017 010237RP

Library of Congress Cataloging-in-Publication Data
Nunn, Daniel.
Inside or outside : where's Eddie? / Daniel Nunn.
p. cm.—(Hide and seek)
Includes bibliographical references and index.
ISBN 978-1-4109-4713-0 (hbk.)
ISBN 978-1-4109-4719-2 (pbk.)
1. Vocabulary—Juvenile literature. I. Title.
PE1449.N775 2012
428.1—dc23 2012000356

Acknowledgments
We would like to thank the following for permission to reproduce photographs: Shutterstock pp.5 (© loriklaszlo), 6 (© Thanida), 7 (© Elnur), 8 (© Kletr), 9 (© Adam Fraise), 10 (© Ihnatovich Maryia), 11, 12 (© tkemot), 13, 14 (© Marteric), 15, 16 (© ansem), 17, 18 (© Ivonne Wierink), 19, 20 (© Patricia Hofmeester), 21 (© jocic), 22 (© WebStudio24h), 23 (© Lois M. Kosch).

Front cover photograph of a tent reproduced with permission of Shutterstock (© vichie81).

Every effort has been made to contact copyright holders of any material reproduced in this book. Any omissions will be rectified in subsequent printings if notice is given to the publisher.

Contents

Meet Eddie the Elephant 4
Inside 6
Outside 8
Find Eddie! 10
True or False? 21
Answers and More! 24

Be careful when you hide!
Eddie can hide in places where people can't. Hiding inside things can be very dangerous. Always ask an adult if it is safe first.

Meet Eddie the Elephant

This is Eddie the Elephant.

Eddie loves to play hide and seek!

Inside

Sometimes Eddie hides **inside** things.

When you are **inside** something, you are in it.

Outside

Sometimes Eddie hides **outside** things.

Outside is the opposite of **inside**. When you are **outside** something, you are not in it.

Find Eddie!

Can you find Eddie?
Count to 10, then off you go!

Where is Eddie? Is he **inside** the tent or **outside** the tent?

Eddie is **inside** the tent.

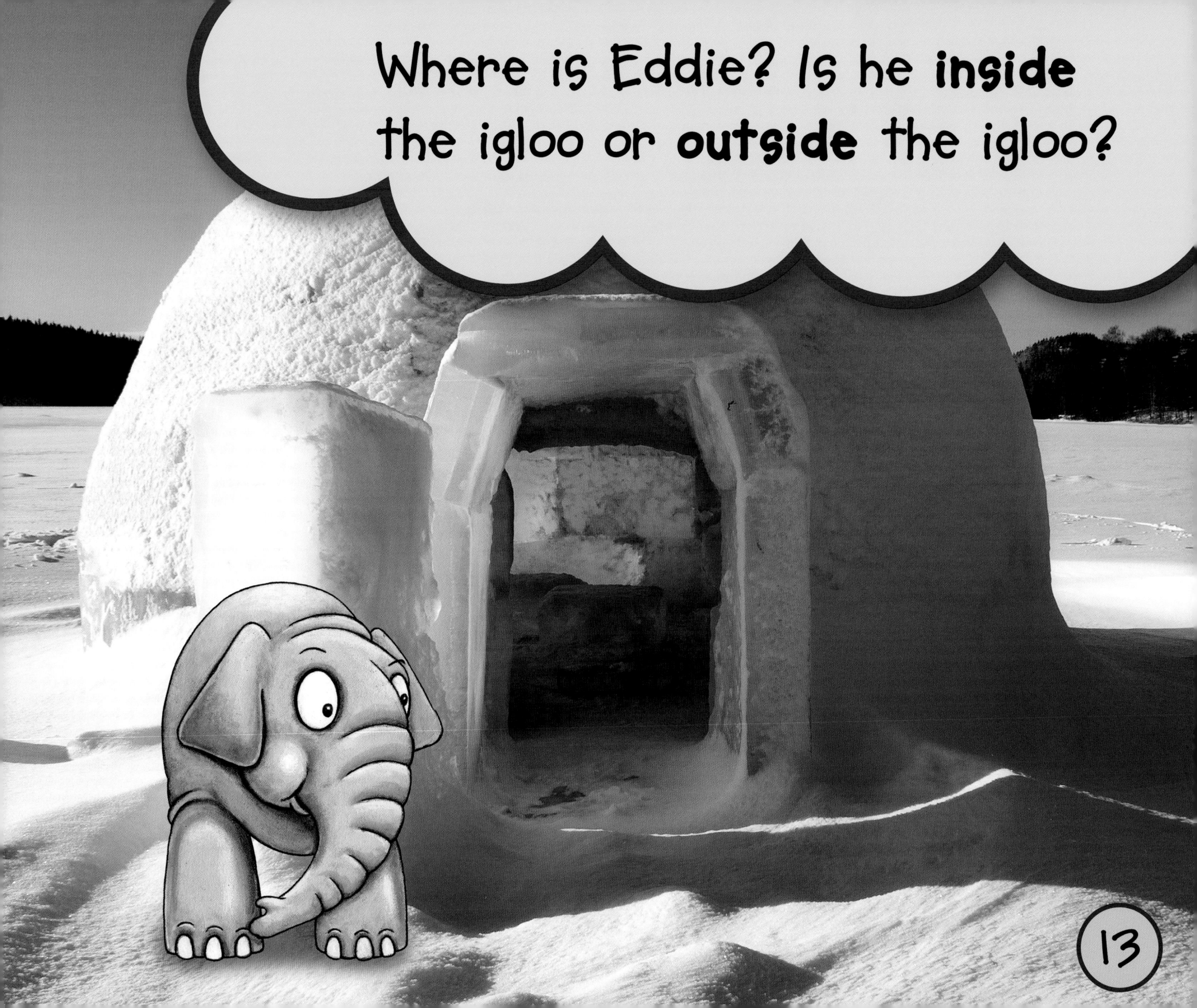
Where is Eddie? Is he **inside** the igloo or **outside** the igloo?

Eddie is **outside** the igloo.

Where is Eddie? Is he **inside** the helicopter or **outside** the helicopter?

Eddie is **inside** the helicopter.

Where is Eddie?
Is he **inside** the cupboard or **outside** the cupboard?

Eddie is **inside** the cupboard.

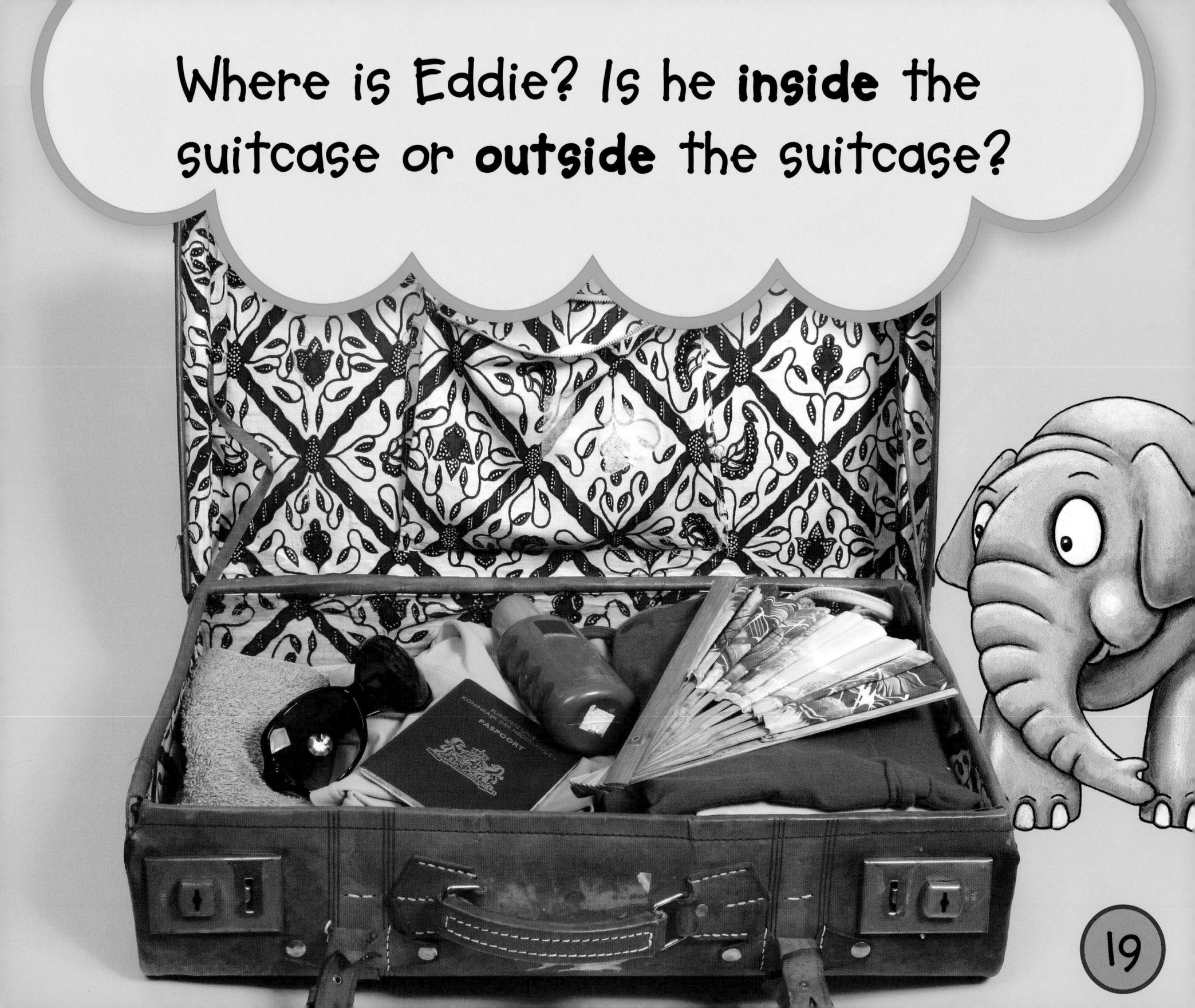
Where is Eddie? Is he **inside** the suitcase or **outside** the suitcase?
PASPOORT

Eddie is **outside** the suitcase.
PASPOORT

True or False?

1. Eddie is **outside** the shoe.
   True or false?

You can find the answers on page 24.

2. Eddie is **inside** the playhouse.
True or false?

3. Eddie is **inside** the rocket.
True or false?

Answers and More!

True or false?

1. False! Eddie is **inside** the shoe.
2. True! Eddie is **inside** the playhouse.
3. False! Eddie is **outside** the rocket.

Where can Eddie hide next?

Look around the room you are in.
What could Eddie hide **inside** of?
What could Eddie hide **outside** of?